Tears Shed With Purpose

poems for a world without concrete

by Samantha Geovjian Clarke

Tears Shed With Purpose: poems for a world without concrete

Copyright © 2018 Samantha Geovjian Clarke

Published and edited by: Wider Perspectives Publishing, which reserves 1ˢᵗ run rights alone, all rights revert to author Samantha Clarke upon delivery

All artist's rights reserved to the author. No part of this publication may be reproduced, distributed, or transmitted in any form or by any means, including photocopying, recording, or other electronic or mechanical methods, without the prior written permission of the author, except in the case of brief quotations embodied in critical reviews and certain other noncommercial uses permitted by copyright law.

And for fuck's sake, don't be all up in this book assuming poems are about you and shit. They aren't (probably). Work of fiction, no persons living or dead, etc.

First Edition:
ISBN: 1720500770
ISBN-13: 978-1720500773
Second Edition **ISBN: 978-1-952773-26-6**

Dedication

For John, who knows why

For Dariel AKA Eayaes, Taz, Samar, Alley, Dan, Alex, Joel, Adam and all my other friends who create—for inspiring me

For the Venue, which opened me

For Anne Michaels, Adrienne Rich, Alice Walker and Sylvia Federici

For everyone who supports me on Patreon and beyond

I

It is starvation
It is bones
It is sleeplessness

The profound alienation of concrete
and clothes

One time, I ate something I had planted
and then pulled out of the ground
and the dirt under my fingernails
didn't even bother me

My mother told me the earth was poisonous

2018

Samantha Geovjian Clarke

Yeah, I'm Fine, Thanks

Oh, don't worry about me, honey--
I can pour fine bourbon out my fingers
if I concentrate and push,
spill inky sapphires onto my notebook,
send time and space both flying
with each pen stroke

therapy, and drugs, and emotional support
are for the wealthy;
I have a pen
and my own soul

trust me, I don't need you

I'm here if you need anything,
you said.

I guess you were worried I'd be torn up
after you ripped me to shreds.

But I have something, and it ain't even a secret.
I have the power to defy pain.
I have DNA that survived a genocide.
I have cells that outlasted an abuser.
I have a body that still cums even after being raped.
I have hips that hold to fat even after starving.
I have a heart that loves, and

I have a pen

2018

II

The forms that history takes--
square, white, concrete--
I long for blood,
for dirt,
for bodies

Pull me in a high tide
to revolution

Anything is better than a terror-dream
of cold, clean, orderly destruction

My *horkur* still lives in the ruins of Aleppo

My heart, and my father's, still
hold the sorrow of atrocity

A man was just murdered in New Orleans;
a woman plowed down by a car in Charlottesville

We are ending, or beginning

Tear it all down. Find *we* and bring me with you.

I will cry and I will bleed with purpose

*For Heather Heyer
and Muhiyidin Moye*

2018

Samantha Geovjian Clarke

Revolutionary

I feel you
like the craters of the moon
on a clear night.

I feel you like the earth below my body
under the sun;
like the
thumping
in my chest
at the top
of a mountain.

I feel you in a way
that should be
ordinary connection, yet--

you are liberation;
a taste of
relief
from a world that polices me
down to my soul.

That regulates even my heart
and the way it loves.

I feel you as water; as sleep;
as wind.

I feel you as nature; a love

as real as the moon

and that alone is
revolutionary.

2017

Samantha Geovjian Clarke

Silver

You spew bitterness
laden with silver--
tongues;
spoons;
bullets.

Betrayal is too kind
and too romantic a word
for the absolute
fucking
over
you proudly slap your name on.

You're not even a sympathetic villain.
Unharmed and unbent,
you lack wholeness
all on your own.
You eat compassion for breakfast;
chew it up and swallow it down.
Take in nutrition and give back shit.

One day your victim
will not be the good you think them,
and you will sleep
with one eye open.

2017

The Old Country

A mountainside of wild irises and cornflowers,
a lamb grazing behind a tattered fence,
a bowl of yogurt and fresh tomatoes
can call through a century of thick time,
drooping with the weight of atrocity--
and longing.
And can I listen?
The heart knows where the body has never been.

2016

Tears Shed With Purpose

What does your flesh mean?
Hips that blend milky into your hungry stomach,
legs that move like a man but hold up
the body of a creature akin to rivers.
And not lazy rivers,
but the hard rush of the Colorado
or the Shenandoah after a thunderstorm.

What does your body mean?
Eyes of a clear winter morning
pull into me, past the years, centuries
of rigid atomization,
your voice like poetry listens, sees

You mean
the scent of freedom,
not the flag-waving Wild West
every-man-for-himself American Constitution
lie
but the reality of human bonding;
of tears shed with purpose;
of what love could possibly mean
in a world without concrete.

and this is why when you are far from me,
my heart-string,
you mean terror
and the realization of what I cannot live without.

2018

III

You are not only blues,
but browns,
and greens,
and deep jewel reds.

You slip golden yellow threads
into your thick, bubbling river run;
the sun reflecting not upon your surface,
but through your depths.

You do not dance.
But it would be a mistake to say you do not move.

What is the difference between what we mean and who we are?

You are the trickling sound of a trumpet on a cool, clear night,
  and I long to stop
  and listen.

2017

Unfitting

I was born, unexpected,
loved desperately
and stubbornly--
not quite out of spite,
but almost, and hard to explain another way
when every single person looked at me,
and her, with something between
suspicion and disdain--

unfitting, unexpected, dark
a child of the Caucasus
with a father who would have been an
unwelcome husband, son
but who--worse--didn't even try

She only hated him because they wanted her to.

instead, she loved me

2018

IV

Can love really be
so simple as this?

Two sets of ears seeking one another's heartbeats?

And for what purpose?

To know it is there,
to know it is there.

2016

To See, In Five Parts

I used to think I couldn't wear seafoam green
but then I looked down at my sun-smoked skin
against the ocean

the earth looks good on everyone

how could I have told you
that you didn't like my body the right way;
that I wanted you to look at me more the way he does

how can you teach someone how to see you

how can someone teach you how to see yourself

--

I screamed *see me*
into what I did not realize
at the time
was a nearly-perfect void

Once, or twice, I saw you as you were--
a crumpled, terrified child--
and even then, you couldn't see me.

I hid from you, and in that way
I abandoned you,
even though I stayed

But you had abandoned me
from the very beginning
--

I understand you,
you whose eyes blink out the messages
shooting through your nerve endings,
you with the twinkle of energy
pulsing in your toes at the peak
of a long conversation,
you whose heart throbs and moans
loudly behind that thin skin.

I can see you,
unintentionally
and unexpectedly open

because we vibe on the same plain, man

and I know that you, like me,
don't know why

I understand you, and both
for your ease and to relieve
this odd drive within me
I mean for you to understand me.

I want to make myself naked before you.

I want to carefully slice apart this chest
and pull with both hands
until you can see

and maybe you can tell me who I am

--

Every time, I am surprised
by hands that feel so alike

but bodies are not as diverse as spirits
and I am open to touch

one night, I slept next to him
and dreamt casually that it was your arm
draped over me

I know you the same, and different

--

What were you gazing into, if it was not me,
when my eyes drifted into yours
and your hair lit at its ends
like a halo

I'm afraid of mattering
I told you,
my heart overturning itself
at the thought of my burdens

You do, and you might
you told me,
and in that moment,
I believed you understood
what it is to be salt

but you, and your voice, are made of silver

2018

V

This world will leave you
scarred

it will hurt to fight

but the fight
is your own

as much
as the pain is

2018

Skin

I used to break out in hives

itchy little reminders, alarm bells
all over my chest, neck and cheeks
when you kissed me

What does the body tell us when we aren't
      listening?

You pulled me out of knowing,
smashed my eyes
and my mind into meal
told my ears they only misheard
even taught my body how to make itself small.

But you couldn't trick my skin

2018

VI

Whatever happens, I have had
the ends of your soft hair brush my nose
as your body pushed deep into mine,
knowing it could find me there
and searching desperately.

I have shaken   trembled
gazed into you
bare
opened my soul and let you see me look
at the scream and the crumbling
faced you and said
I don't know anything that I know

Whatever happens, I have held your hand

Whatever happens, I and you know
at least
that someone else knows what might happen,
what has happened,
what has happened to us.
What has happened, or might happen, to you
to me
to us all

Whatever happens, you and I have seen one another
and you and I have seen outward
with the same eyes.

2018

VII

Poems that begin, or end, with questions
take hold of the reins--
rein me in, like a well-trained animal
because I have no grounds to make statements

who am I to understand
what, and how, and especially why

well, I've never taken a class or anything
I say in apology
for my hard-earned folk training
and intuition

you do, and you might, matter
is the truest statement I have ever heard
from a person who believed
she had to make them for me

but didn't she?

does ability matter in the face of perception?

2018

Condescending
this is for you, The Internet

I just think it's funny how

okay, first of all

you're doing great, sweetie

2018

1917

I am from a world of unfitting,
more even than my sister
with her blue eyes, her Subaru,
her sweet little boy with the pale hair

even though neither of us believes in God

I stand brown and sturdy.
My back is held straight, consciously,
but it still sends a clear and contradicting message--
these stooped shoulders will carry your weight

My ancestors taught me, eventually,
how to eat and what to do about
all this hair,
but even they had to start almost from scratch
after 1917.

I am defined by
unfitting
by the way the world reacts--has reacted--
to my body,
and to my life

The past still exists, and the future
and I have no choice but to be

2018

Consume Without Becoming

What odd, horrific kind of hunger
comes from overconsumption;
false wealth like a knockoff handbag
while the rich wear impoverished thinness
like a fashion statement.

I have spent my life in a ricochet
between too much and not enough food,
between overweight and malnourished,
bones or fat, but never muscle--
never sinews, organs, energy, meat

I have always starved

Women know what it is to starve.
I know it in my veins
and my ancestors whisper it to me in my sleep.
I must be more
and I must be less
and I must consume without becoming.
I must fill myself for the past
and I must empty myself to survive.

And they tell us we are lucky

My nana was from the third world
and she made us all look poor

2018

VIII

I am fallin'
I am fallin'
I am fallin' for you
But you like them fallen
You like them fallen
You like them broken in two

2015

Utility

What is kind, that I am not of it?
I slipped so easily into position
as nanny, housekeeper, secretary
because I'd already spent my whole life being
pulled into the inner circles
and then ignored.

You have to *learn* how
to be properly used.

And I have learned, so deeply
that like a pet
I crave only to sit at the feet
of that kind, which I am not,
and be honored by my own utility.

--

How does a body learn that it is not
its own?

I had thought for so long
that it was you who taught it--
you, who giveth and taketh away
food
and whose years of touch began
under coercion--

but mine knew long before it knew you.

This body, these arms, belong to Mrs. Potter,
who can't clean her own toilets,
and these legs belong to Dr. Foster,

who can't bring food to his own party.
These lungs belong to Nina and Ray,
who need flute lessons,
and this cunt belongs to every man who wants it.

These shoulders belong to anyone who leans on them.

Is my heart, and my soul, my own?

--

You made a mockery of my mind,
after he made it a war zone.

Has the world not possessed you
as it has me?

I had believed you wanted my truth,
my soul, or what was left of it,
but your kind, which I am not,
looks for utility. And I am of use.

You make me believe
I am nothing more.

2018

Being a Lesbian Doesn't Fix Anything

Now I gotta look suspicious at women too,
you know.
And yeah, because of you.
I saw Sylvia Federici speak one time--
you didn't come, at the last minute--
and she said in this world,
even love between lesbians is perverse.
I guess I shoulda listened.
I know better than to fling myself too quickly
into a romance with anyone with a penis--
I don't leap without looking.
But damn if I wasn't fully charmed by
that coiled hair, long legs, bouncy walk
and that goddamn accent.
Was it that spoon turned your tongue silver?
I'm dead sick of these eyes
being missed for their seeing
and of the way your kind--
which I am not--finds me useful.
Useful or pitiful, or both;
your guilt projected on me
either way
and my body a thing
either way.
Dead.
Sick.
It's especially *something*, from you,
whom I brought into brown
the way you brought me into queer;
each of us soothing the other--
feel comfortable in your identity.
But you found the one difference
and made it everything.
What is kind, that I am not of it,

I wonder in my lowest moments
thinking of you;
thinking of the way you believe I was
"born into this world"
and the way you engage with him
like I am his dependent.
I am not his child, or yours,
and I was born into this world myself;
alone, more than anything,
and definitely not in need
of you.

2018

IX

How ugly a contradiction
that love and cruelty can take the same form
speak with the same voice
look out through the same hot-and-cold hazel eyes.

I wish I could say

he never loved me

he was never anything but cruel

his heart was cold

but I remember too many times
you held my tenderness in your hands,
kissed it gently
and placed it carefully back into my chest.

If god blessed me,
he would steal your kindnesses from me
and leave only the wrongs.

Then, perhaps, I could forget you in peace.

2016

X

You, whom I cannot call mine
because the blue freedom of you
I love -
you, whom I fear to tell
that I am yours,
whose liquid animal body
sings praises to mine
even as it presses

What kind of love
would not provide the pain that heals

You, whose intangible realness
pulls me into knowing,
into knowing what I know

You fragment and fill me
sift and smooth and strengthen.

You, whom I cannot but love,
I learn again each moment.

2018

XI

We all have dreams of the war now,
of fascists or of terror
or perhaps, of brother facing sister--
a new kind of civil war
that doesn't forget women will fight too.

Mine aren't even nightmares anymore.
They're too much old news,
like the dystopian horrors of the DMV;
the dentist; high school
that we all just laugh and call
stress dreams.

I have stress dreams about holocausts.

It is not even death that I smell in the air;
we are already mostly dead--
it is cold, bitter helplessness
and dread

will we even be enough of a threat
to fear torture, interrogation, exile?

Or should I be more afraid
of easy extermination

2018

Freedom

A rainbow of genders floods through me

I am all
I feel all
I love all

I crash through drywall to leave my house instead of using the door

I decorate myself with all the yesterdays and tomorrows of the human spirit

I have a soul that can fly

What unprecedented freedom this is

2015

Los Pobres de la Tierra

The trouble is not
that you won't let me love you;
your heart opens to my poetry
and, though tender, your skin moves
to my touch.

Your hands become firm
when they touch me.

No, sweet love, you do not
push me away.

Instead, you pull
with all the possession
of your father, and his kind,
upon my soul--
my soul, which submits
but which will never be possessed.

Do you see me? Do you see
my earth-skin, my strength
and my ingenuity?
Or am I a fascinating venture
into the world of *los pobres de la tierra*;
a world you claim to respect
but which you yet stand above?

You are the very thing you most criticize,
and I love you in a way that you do not love me.

2018

We

The mysterious *you,* they,
a sense in the liver
and the stomach that there is somewhere a *we*
that we do not understand

We are shattered

And it is *we* that we struggle to find,
before it is too late

2018

A Man Who Left His Niece Behind

You died sudden, swift and shocking,
your story on national news

how the wing just *fell* off the plane
and you spiraled into a death-crash
like in some action movie

even dying you couldn't do by halves

and I have been afraid to write you poems,
even though you have come to me,
reassured me,
welcomed my niece to the stars, my little bird,
and asked my mother to tell me.

Even in death, you have still been my father.

You have always known that I couldn't do it alone.

Can you forgive me for taking six years
to put you in ink,
which I have done for countless almost-lovers
but not for you?

It's just one more thing
I couldn't do without you

2018

XII

We fell--
moon, stars, heaven and earth--
at once.

Not one after another,
doubt-clad and insecure,
but together, as one momentous occurrence.

This soul, which I laid bare before you,
saw in yours the starlight of an age;
the intelligent twinkle of recognition;
the spark of movement that only grand forces of nature carry.

And you saw, in mine,
something grounded and warm,
which both encircled you and called for
your encirclement.

We have met one another face to face
and, somehow,
already arm in arm.

We shook hands, locked eyes,
and faced love together,
fingers entwined.

What meaning there is in these words!
You--comrade, companion, and partner--
stand by my side, and I by yours.

2017

XIII

It is the time of that
almost-winter tree-fall
when the leaves have turned
halfway to mud

and I have almost decided
if I can really remember
one specific instance
or if everything
about you and I was rape.

After all,
if the mind has been broken
and stolen,
how can the body not be?

Our bodies know
when we lie to them.

Will the mud and muck and deterioration
I feel damp upon my soul
mean death, or rebirth?

I feel, on days like these,
that I have nothing left to give.

I feel only the hollow, scooped-out feeling of a person

entered, and drained, and

I can only make love if
it is made for me.

I give myself,
but still to be taken.

I feel sometimes
that I will never know
another way.

And this is when my heart breaks:
I cannot heal
because I was never granted a wound.

I cannot become a survivor
if I was never a victim.

I reach for more
and more pain;
more harm;
more fear,

just to feel I deserve some compassion.

Just to be seen, picked up, stroked
with validating fingers
and told
you're safe now. You can heal.

Just to paint a clearer picture
than a half-muddy mess
of leaves upon the pavement,
stepped in and never
rescued.

2017

Commenter on a Feminist Blog
Thanks, Knucklehead

You feminists are all alike
Women like you are the reason that intelligent men
    become misogynists
I've evolved past modern feminism's incredibly
    narrow-minded, uncompromising, and
    shrill approach to issues
This discussion does nothing but demonize men
You are all delusional
Indoctrination!
Find one law that discriminates against black
    people
The "racist" person was the most level-headed
    person there
If you're gay, black, or a woman people are scared
    to fire you
Cis white male? Christian? Nobody worries or even
    can conceive that we might be
    discriminated against
Can you womansplain that to me?
I think it's awful that you really believe that men
    have oppressed women throughout
    history
Have a little respect
I think feminism has largely been a tool of the elite
    to destroy families
In the bedroom most still prefer a man to take
    charge

You're only playing the victim as a cheap rhetorical
    trick
Most women would be happier if they were
    housewives

Feminists target vulnerable people and give them
    an enemy to blame all of their problems on.
The PATRIARCHY!
Stop playing the victim. Your hurt feelings are not
    an argument.
Men's problems are not sufficiently listened to by
    society as a whole, women in general,
        and especially by feminists
Do you want people to just say attagirl?
You're fighting against human nature and natural
    selection

2015

XIV

I, having been torn,
pull apart knowing
to look at terror;
to dig into the doubt
that peels us away
beneath.

I open a channel
into the scream that sits
heavy, in the bottom
of the stomach.
In it, there is a truth,
or at least an absence of falsehood.

We are missing.

Yet there is we
in the scream itself.

2018

XV

It is only mysterious
how lithe curl and curve
fit neatly into your
summer-in-the-Carolinas body,
the contradictory strength and frailty
of a daisy-stem
as you exude sunlight
from your fingertips.

Can your hands touch my warmth
the way they touch my palms,
my temples, the curve of my back?

I must meet you again each day.
Ever-changing yet stable force,
you take the shape of your soul
in any given moment.

I reach, and am met with the feeling
that I am already there.

2018

Pyro

It's dangerous to be a pyro
when you are made of earth.
Your fire excited me as it plowed through my forests,
burning off old underbrush
and lighting me in a way
edging on unnatural.
But in the end, that Aries fire burnt me too deeply,
and I could no longer let you free in me
or else be consumed.

2015

XVI

A small bundle of wildflowers were cradled in her arms.
I watched her as she got off the bus,
my heart stealing
away to whatever moment those flowers were meant for.

I breathed deeply as I passed the church gardens,
a momentary double-take of nature and religion.
It would have to do.

I told you, last night, that in another life
I would have had your child.

These days, we take romance in shots.

Will a day come when we can no longer make room for love?
We gulp it down,
because our bodies know the answer
to that question.

2017

XVII

With you, I sacrifice myself to my past
on my own terms,
look into your winter eyes
with all the fear and fawning
I had to hide from him,
slide my body under your thumb
and cry *please*

I whisper my humiliations in the moonlight,
scream my pain into your hand,
 sob   whimper   tearlessly, into your ear--
 and you listen, hear me, soothe me with your hard hands
 and your teeth

With you, I suffer
the way I want to, must, suffer

like digging out a splinter
we make the wound worse to heal it

I suffer by my own hand, yours;
the future will have my mark upon it
in place of his

2018

XVIII

What pull do you have
upon the fibers of the muscles
within my chest;
what bypass have you made
directly to my insides;
what insidious hideout have you built
in my lungs, my heart, my liver?

Why do you grasp hold of my throat
without even looking me in the eye?

Years; miles; ages
reduce to minutes
when you slip past me,
pull for just a moment,
and are gone.

What are you made out of?

I fear it is
too much love.

2017

Birds Wings

Your fingers touched me like
a bird's wings
touch
the sun.

Angles of perception can be
the difference between
passion and indifference,
kindness and coldness,
affection and competition--
and I don't know whose angle
was obtuse.

I know only that I reached for you
to see you,
and you reached for me
to have me.

2015

Regrets

Lethargically vibrant regrets
Flawless laughter
A magic eightball
Fucking in the back of a 2 by 4 pickup
She, soulless
Me, inept

2015

XIX

Angle to angle,
long to short,
two ends of a spectrum
and, between us,
four points of nature.

Wholeness.

Is this what they speak of
with their talk of halves
and becoming one?

But I am no half a person,
and you—larger than the sky—
are certainly whole alone.

We must, then,
be not two halves of one
but two wholes making
something entirely new;
something that has all the power
of the earth itself behind it.

We are Uranus and Gaia,
who together created life.
We are Prometheus and Athena,
who together formed humanity.

You outpour, and I unearth,
and creation blooms forth.

No, we do not complete one another.
Together, we are nature's completeness.

2017

XX

Not only did you need liquor
to enter me;
to edge away the anxious thumping
and put yourself inside me,

you refused to bond.

You kept one last shield up
even to me,
not for safety, but for distance.

This was love?
This seeming ease that was yet covered
with a thin sheen
of nervous hiddenness?

How can I believe you loved me
if you did not want me?
If you turned away
from the sacred bond of sex?

And worse still, though you did not want me,
you wanted no part of me if you could not have all.

You were like a child who only cares about a toy
as long as no other children can play with it.

2017

Portland, years later

Grey skies, cold
nights and depression

a city filled with people who live
like bad poets--
isolated, dreary

I long for the sunshine
where people are rude and care about each other;
where people care what other people think about
who they are
not how

but stillness is vanishing
and my life's work depends
upon movement

2018

XXI

Easily, words form into beauty
and truth
when the daylight trickles from your light eyes
and my thoughts weigh like pebbles
in your presence.

You tell me you are unromantic
and don't think to bring flowers,
but you make me a gift of your rawest thoughts;
you present your mind's process as an offering
like a poem.

How deeply linked are logic and feeling!
And we make them inextricable.

Touch me with your heart,
explain to me with your hands,
make love to me with your ideas.

We are as simple as the moon
and as complex as the way we hold one another's eyes
and see.

2017

Reach

Is there straining within that bone cage your ribs make,
or has your heart stilled, so soon,
the emptiness of the shoreline when the moon pulls its waves away?
I cannot tell whether I meet resistance or nothingness when I reach.
The brick wall or the black hole;
The barrier or the vacuum?
I can hope only that the reachings themselves are not empty,
void of neither intention nor result.
Because you have a set of dimples, a bend in your hip bones, a flint in your brown eyes
that I must reach for.

2015

Showers

In South Carolina,
the rain does not fall as a matter of course
upon cobblestones and churches
(lined with a thin sheen of eerie cleanliness)
but heavy, sudden
and serious, a cleansing necessitated
by the way sin sits in its bones.

It has begun to rain harder
and more rarely in Portland.

The scientists say *climate change!*
as if the earth needing stricter cleanses weren't
exactly the same thing.
But I know.
I can feel her wincing
as she showers herself in agony.

There was once excruciating beauty
and wild freedom here

2018

The Sins of Virginia do Visit Only in Winter

It is impossible to remember the sins of a place--
or to blame the land,
a victim itself, in a way--
when spring releases honeysuckle through every pore, and
  when mint grows wild between stones,
  the grandchildren of an ancient ocean floor.
  There are too many births to remember the dyings;
  too much moss quilted over the old battle earthworks,
  too much love in every new mama bird, deer, rabbit and bear,
  to remember that once slaves toiled to make that mint-bearing soil produce acre after acre of tobacco,
  that trees still living were once unwilling hangmen's posts,
  that good men--thousands of them--died here fighting for evil.
  That walnut and pine, just fifty years ago, still held firm
  occupation of the countryside,
  before men's greed
  so fully overtook us all.
  But forgetfulness is a Virginian spring trait.
  The barren winter closes her heart to joy and,
  once again,
  the bleakness is remembered.
  And winter is just long enough,
  every year,
  for sobriety--
  and never quite long enough for change.

2015

XXII

Through joys and tragedies,
despite the understanding of a love honest and warm,
I still
feel you.

How is it that you occupy centuries
in a heart that has never felt your touch?

You gave no joy, no meaning,
no love
and yet, your soul still calls to mine,
as though we were entwined.

You never wanted me in word, but somehow,
I feel the ache of you across time and space
and I know I cannot answer.

I still feel you, though I cannot believe you ever felt me.

2017

Fat

Tofu fried in coconut oil.
Just a little bit of fat;
fat that belonged on my bones.
Fat you melted off of them
with your icy glare
and your wild, uneven heartbeat.
Fat that took up space;
that had once dared to exist
and had left me
to deal with the winter on my own.

Fat that I needed on my organs.
Fat as a protective barrier
around my heart.

I consumed fat--just a little
bit of fat--
as an insistence on my right
to have form
and tangibility.
I slipped behind you carefully,
in the shadows.
I knew my defiant act of existence
must be a secret.

You found out about the tofu
fried in coconut oil.
But it was too late.
I had already built enough onto myself
to shed you.

2017

Fear

My fear
is their sensationalism.
That moment I realized others who craft words
    into
meaning,
into
truth,
are not looking for my fear or my story,
but for the same sell
as every other capitalist enterprise,
that moment, I was betrayed.

Not the towering testaments of this capitalism
crashing in a puff of gray
nor the cries of fellow citizens
nor the t e r r o r we all spit off our tongues
caused my fear,
but

the news flashes of mobs swarming
men in turbans
women in hijabs
children with great black eyes just like my mirror
the way they looked like the torch-bearing swarm
    from
Beauty and the Beast
but not against a misunderstood monster,
just
people who looked like me,
who had the misfortune of living among
whiteness
with my brown skin and my thick eyebrows and

my thick hair and
my dark eyes and
the coffee and dance and music and language of
    my
people.
Just people.

My fear is the war on ...is terror another word for
    fear?
the news reports of soldiers who died
making jokes about warheads on foreheads
and calling me a terrorist
(just kidding).
Not reported—a child set on fire in
    Al-Mahmudiyah, Iraq
by her rapists:
five American soldiers.

My fear is watching three men slashed
with a knife in front of you
for daring to defend you
from a violent white supremacist,
like two girls on a train
a mile and a half from my home.

My fear is the children slaughtered for their brown
    skin
and for beautiful clothes upon their heads
and for the taste of the languages of water and
    flowers
and for the music of sunsets
and for speaking like my brother
and for dancing like my horkur
and for looking like me.

2017

XXIII

What rose-colored warmth trails
along my spine
following the riverbed your fingers make?

And my own fingers,
finding your ridges to climb
and explore,
adventurers in a strange but familiar terrain.

How do two souls, meeting, become bodies?

You unfold.
you are not aspen, but birch;
not branch, but bough.
Not a wave, but a current.

And I, too, unearth myself,
opening to your sunlight.

We are Pluto and Mercury;
thoughts and words;
water and earth.

We are the crash of a waterfall
plunging into a cavern;
a river run rushing
down a mountainside;
a thunderstorm
in a forest.

We are bodies, and we are souls,
and we will be free.

2017

New Words

Those freakish fingers creep through the fourth
            dimension
to prod at me,
time itself no barrier
to the inflictions you insist upon.

I overturn stones,
like a fool,
and find all the mold and insects
I should have expected.

Of course it was you.

Of course it always was.

I have had to learn new words
to understand what you did to me.

2018

XXIV

I doubt you ever knew
how in those years that followed,
when I was alive only in the time between when he
    fell asleep
and when I did,
your fingers again brushed my skin so tenderly--
you, whom I hardly knew.

I doubt you ever knew, because
to you, gentle caressing was just
something you did on a date

it certainly wasn't a landslide
or an earthquake;
the mass movement of earth when it finally stirs

but

for me, I held to it like a memorial

you have had tenderness I told myself
to soothe
with the same tone of voice people used with my
    aunt
when her husband died.

you have had tenderness I whispered to myself,
lying next to my sleeping husband
and remembering what a caress felt like

2018

XXV

I nestle into memories,
quietly feeling the presence of old existence,
evidenced by carpet-tears and layered paint
and a sometimes-stirring in a still room.

I live in these memories,
alone,
safely sequestered among others who
know the illumination of aloneness,
sad but shining.

Lingerings of a gentle, resigned affliction
nudge my senses in the stillness--
who, here, once loved?--
and I feel a companionship that soothes
my own aching heart.

We all, though solitary, sense that we are not alone,
for the heart that loves reaches through time itself
for another heart to see it.

2016

Man, Can She Paint

God, he's beautiful
out the corner of my eye

that sweatshirt and shorts look like
bright, royal red robes
when what I'm really looking at
is her poetry.

I find words,
but she paints them.

She talks of her skin like cocoa and cinnamon,
starbursts and Saturn,
and all I can say about mine is
olives

I can't paint, but shit,
at least I can see,
because I bet you no one's ever looked at that guy before
and seen a princess in glorious robes

she gets into my eyes

maybe she can help me look in the mirror

2018

Solidarity Ain't an Abstract Concept

Damn right it's wisdom, and
damn right it's philosophy,
this talk of love and spirits and poverty;
this music about gangsters and police;
this poetry about skin
and babies

Maybe I apologize for myself too much,
but you better get it out your head
that I'll ever apologize for them,
they who understand soul - *my soul* -
and aren't afraid to say it

It's a simple lesson: *open your heart*

make some fucking noise

sing along, for once

try shouting and screaming,
making some trouble.
Practice *shoulder to shoulder*
and maybe you'll learn

it's a simple lesson

2018

Dialectical

Time tugs, or pushes, or
perhaps both

I learned a new word--*dialectical*--
I think it's useful here
because

my ancestors seem to be both trying to tell me
something
and asking me a question;
and I feel
we are distinct stages of one sameness:

humanity, perhaps, or maybe something narrower;
a tradition of memory and of understanding;
a grounded *something* that connects us
and bonds us with anyone who is, and
understands, salt

In you, I recognize salt, despite the presence of a
very foreign
and alluring synthetic material;
LSD perhaps, or aspartame,
a perfect and eerie version
of the imperfection nature produces.

You are not simple.

Can you understand what my ancestors
want me to know, or want to know?

I am salt, onions, phosphorus;
the things of the earth
and you are the scientific perfecting
of their elements.

We must understand one another
or perish. Or worse--
fail.

2018

Objective

I am subject; you are object
objective: be less alone

You are so lonely.

Me? I'm lonely sometimes.
I can love you

will loving you
evoke love in return?

I will never ask.

Can subject and object
lose their distinction,
become a together-entity
and meet the objective?

We will both, still,
come away lonely

2018

Small Monstrosity

I have become a small monstrosity,
soaked in the tepid humility of the battered
and parading my littleness in hope—
false, desperate—
of being seen, and then overlooked.
Me?
Little old unobtrusive me?
Surely I am no threat to your—
what is it this time?
Manhood? Whiteness? Family values?
Pay no mind to my large brown eyes.
They are the stereotype of the meek; the veiled,
and not of the brilliant, the bearded, or the terrible.
I do not represent an ancient,
impossibly resilient people, nor do I represent
the terrifying strength of womanhood.
I am no creature of sexual intuition, or of sight.
I am only a small being
in a small frame,
with the intellect of a sweet cow
and the strength of a kitten.
I hold no wild, radical, intelligent ideas;
no density in my bones;
no fearless endurance in my heart.
No history in my soul.
I am the ugliness of cute;
the weakness of pretty.
The lie of a wide-eyed, girlish charm.
Pay me no mind.
I am only small.

2018

XXVI

When in my bones
I sense deeply the still-pulling flesh and blood
and agony

and in my beating heart
I feel sadness that lays heavy, settled,
always weighing at the bottom
and carried around until
I almost forget it is there;

when time falls, dripping slowly
like wax from a candle
and holds within it the
lingerings of atrocity--

I must wonder if it is memory
or visitation.

I know what I am remembering.
But does it belong to those who came before me,
showing me what they felt
and knew
and lost?

Or is it time; history; circumstance itself
calling to me through the thickness
of my earth-hewn body;
through the way a soul remembers more
than a life does?

I do not know who this pain
belongs to.

2017

XXVII

My love songs to the mountains
are swept up
by a southeastern wind, coming off the ocean to
bring my lyrics
to where they belong--
the echoes and valleys of the Columbia majesties.

But no sooner does that wind pick up my voice
than it is
lost
in a vehicular rush,
the whiteness
that millions of people in living machines
becomes.

My voice is lost, and my praises unheard,
and I
continue to sing.

2015

Women Have Always Known

What you do not understand, she said,
is that women have always known.

We have always known what is necessary,
how to wake at dawn and set the kettle,
how to nurse a child and debate a philosopher.

We have always known how to do what is
necessary with compassion.

We know how to sing to a sink full of dishes,
how to wail and mourn,
how to demand bread and praise the sun and
decorate our hair and
how to overthrow kings and presidents.

We have always known.

Women, we who are defined by what we are not,
are salt

we are bread, we are ground, we are fire and tears

if you do not hold us back, we will go to the front,
and that is what frightens you

We, women, know our mother.
You know her only the way you know us:
how to take from and bore into;

what she gives and how to tame her.

We know about volcanoes.

Women have always known about volcanoes.
We have always known about landslides and
earthquakes,
   tsunamis and hurricanes,
   floods and ice ages.

Become us. You are not our opposite.
We are low, but we are nearer the earth.

2018

XXVIII

The project is humanity

We watched the driver,
gloved, put Jeff's coat in a plastic bag
before putting it in the ambulance behind him.
Tasha called Jeff a bum,
but when she saw that, she said
"well that's degrading."

What we're fighting for is each other

In 1905, the Bolsheviks began forming workers' clubs all over Russia,
  which were initially political in nature,
  but quickly came to include art, song,
  math and physics classes
  alongside political speeches and organizing.
  It worked because regular people understand
  how much self and other are connected.

To feel you is revolutionary

  One time, between jobs, when the food stamps weren't enough,
  a comrade I'd never met, from another organization, another tendency,
  another city sent me 200 dollars
  and just said "it's good praxis."

We forget, sometimes, the humanity of *we;*
the poetry of our struggle;
the beauty of *side by side*

and *united*
and the raw, emotional power
of a battle cry.

The project *is* humanity.
It is both humanity and *our humanity*
that we fight for.

2018

XXIX

Show me who I am

this unfitting soul has never had a community;
a family,
to teach it what and how to be

so it grasps at bystanders like
you clutched at your mama's skirt

What does my skin mean

give me a language that isn't colonized,
anything but *ethnic, exotic, olive*

feed me foods that melt on my tongue,
sit firm in my belly,
radiate through my eyes

play me music for hips to move to

make me clothes for curves, and movement,
with colors of the earth
and fine, sturdy threads

put oil in my hair and kohl around my eyes

paint me, dress me, feed me
give me air to breathe
and then please,
put me in front of a mirror

2018

XXX

Your heartbeat is steady and even-
such a strange comfort
after the knockings-about of his,
thumping around in his chest like it wanted out
as much as I did.

It is indescribably unsettling
to place your head upon a man's breast,
tenderly and restfully,
and be met with the eerie off-beat pounding
of his untamed insides-

A terrific mayhem he-
we-
mistook for wildness
and freedom.

But there is more freedom to be found
in rhythm
than in mayhem.

2015

The Defiant Need Witchcraft

I saw her eyes the most shadowed
I'd ever seen them
when she asked me if it was too late for us.
Have we already been too broken,
she asked me,
because she knew I could feel the bottom
and--not her kind--could tell the truth.

I told her they could never take our bodies
which meant we'd always have something to fight for.
But I felt, in the hollow of my liver, two things:

perhaps they *could* take our bodies and

still, we might not fight for them.

I didn't tell her the truth, because
the truth is that I don't know.

All I can feel, here at the bottom, is the collective terror-scream
of a people not only wounded, but blind
and who know they are blind.

We all are.

And I begin to see why the defiant need witchcraft, or religion;
why revolutionaries divide and communes fall.

What hope is there in anything but faith
that we still have a soul left?

There is no program, no party, no movement
without the kind of stirring only
the human soul can do.

2018

ABOUT THE AUTHOR

Samantha Geovjian Clarke is a writer, poet, comedian and activist with a penchant for boxed macaroni and cheese, Vladimir Lenin and anything Jack White touches with his magical fingers. She can be found on the staff at the Unpopular Opinion comedy podcast network as well as on Twitter @comicwisdom and Patreon as SamanthaClarke.

Her first poetry book, *The Knowing of Being Loved*, is available on Amazon.

If you have praise, ideas, or booking requests you can contact Samantha through one of her many social media profiles.

If you have complaints, you can contact the complaint department. Of Macy's or something, I don't know. We don't have one.

♥

colophon

Brought to you by Wider Perspectives Publishing, care of Tanya Cunningham-Jones and James Wilson with the mission of advancing the poetry and creative community of Hampton Roads, Virginia.

See our production of the works of
    Terra Leigh
    Tanya Cunningham (Scientific Eve)
    Ray Simmons
    Taz Waysweete'
    Bobby K. (The Poor Man's Poet)
    J. Scott Wilson (TEECH!)
    Jorge Mendez & JT Williams
    Sarah Eileen Williams
    Jason Brown (Drk Mtr)
    Lisa M. Kendrick
    Ken Sutton (the Bard of Machipongo)
    the Hampton Roads Artistic Collective
and others to come soon.

We promote and support the artists of the 757
    from the seats, from the stands,
    from the snapping fingers and clapping hands
    from the pages, and the stages
    and now we pass them forth to the ages
(Stop it James, just stop it!)

Check for the above artists on FaceBook, the Virginia Poetry Online channel on YouTube, and the Hampton Roads Artistic Collective webpage.
Hampton Roads Artistic Collective is the non-profit extension of WPP and strives to simultaneously support worthy causes in Hampton Roads and the creative artists.

www.ingramcontent.com/pod-product-compliance
Lightning Source LLC
LaVergne TN
LVHW021130080426
835510LV00034B/3153